The
Bhutan
Bucket
List

Professor R.K. Marjerison

Dr. Stavan Attwood

PHANTOM PRESS
K E Y W E S T

FOREWORD

Forget everything you know about Bhutan.

It doesn't matter if you are a first time visitor or a native to the kingdom; there is something in this book that will impact your life.

The best parts of Bhutan are not found on any maps. While a visit to the Tiger's Nest shouldn't be missed, the real beauty of Bhutan exists beyond the temples, markets and rice fields. It exists in the people.

The authors of *The Bhutan Bucket List* have immersed themselves in Bhutanese culture for several years. What follows may at first appear to be a simple list, but it is so much more. Each item is a primer for a new adventure or cultural experience. Each has a purpose. More importantly, each one of them provides a damn good excuse to really interact with the people of Bhutan, and in doing so to create memories that last a lifetime. It is in such experiences that the magic of Bhutan can be found.

Enjoy the Bucket List and the adventure it gives you!

- David L. Sloan, Key West, March 2015

ACKNOWLEDGEMENTS

The Authors wish to offer their warm thanks to Karma Choden, Phuntsho Wangdi, Mui Mui, Ganchu, Tulku Geduen Pelzang, David Sloan, Joanna James, and all of our friends in Bhutan for making our time here so meaningful and so fulfilling.

ABOUT THE BUCKET LIST

1. No Instruction Manual

There is no shortage of guidebooks and travel memoirs on Bhutan. Some hold your hand and provide great detail every step of the way while others describe a whimsical paradise. This is not one of those books. You know what you like. Consider this a scavenger hunt that you can tailor to your desires. That's the approach we're taking here and once you get a few check marks under your belt, you will understand why.

2. Adventure and Challenge

Some tasks are easy to accomplish, some are difficult, and some are close to impossible. The mix is intended to introduce you to new experiences in an array of locations and help to enhance your Bhutan experience. Bhutan is rapidly changing so many of these activities and experiences will not be possible for future generations of adventurers. Cherish the uniqueness of Bhutan. Don't sweat it if you can't cross an item off. Take things at your own pace and modify them as you desire. No one is grading your performance. This is all about learning, growing, sharing, adventure and most importantly, having fun!

3. Inspiration

We know enough about Bhutan to know that as a 'chillip' or foreigner, one could spend a lifetime in Bhutan and still not truly 'know' or fully understand Bhutan. It's a complex and wonderful land. What we try to do is help you to put yourself in opportunity's way. When it comes to words of wisdom we call in the experts. Shakespeare, Mark Twain, Vincent van Gogh and Buddha are all contributors with quotations that lend an additional layer to each adventure. Some are sappy, some twisted, some appropriate, some perhaps less so, and a few are probably misattributed. Feel free to cross them out and replace them with your own.

4. Respecting the Culture

Bhutan is home to a rich but relatively conservative culture. For this reason, and as when visiting any new country, we ask that you be respectful of local norms, the people, and the natural environment, during your time there.

5. Satisfaction

Whether you tick off every item in this list from 1-100, or only take each journey in your mind from the comfort of your favorite chair, we hope that this book will entertain, amuse, inform, and leave you with a sense of satisfaction. We have worked hard to make this a list that will enhance your time in Bhutan or, at least the time you spend thinking about Bhutan. We want to leave you feeling that the adventures you had checking things off translated into one hell of a bang for your buck. If we were successful, help spread the word on social media, our Facebook page, The Bhutan Bucket List, or website, BhutanBucketList.com and give us a quick 5-star review on Amazon. If we didn't live up to your expectations, e-mail our publisher David Sloan at Phantom Press with your feedback so that we can make it better: **david@phantompress.com**.

5. Glossary

We have used a number of terms in Dzongkha, the national language, in order to retain as much of Bhutan as possible in our writing. While the meaning of these terms should generally be apparent from the descriptions we provide, you can also look them up in the glossary at the back of the book.

Thanks for allowing us to help you experience the magical Kingdom of Bhutan!

The Authors

"Twenty years from now you will be more disappointed by the things that you didn't do than by the ones you did do. So throw off the bowlines. Sail away from the safe harbor. Catch the trade winds in your sails. Explore. Dream. Discover."

- H. Jackson Brown, Jr.

1

BRACE FOR LANDING

Paro International Airport is considered to be the most difficult and challenging commercial international airport in the world, with only a handful of pilots cleared to land or take off. You will see why as the plane slaloms along the valley, the mountainsides almost within touching distance, before making a last turn on its wing-tip only seconds before touchdown. The weightlessness of the descent is like a roller coaster dropping, while taking off will remind you of an Apollo-era rocket launch. Alprazolam (Zanax) is recommended for the faint of heart.

"Up, up the long, delirious burning blue
I've topped the wind-swept heights with easy grace
Where never lark, or ever eagle flew —
And, while with silent, lifting mind I've trod
The high un-trespassed sanctity of space,
Put out my hand, and touched the face of God."

- John Gillespie Magee, Jr.

2

FLY ON THE WINGS OF THE TIGER

The spectacular Taktsang Monastery – known as the Tiger's Nest – is an obligatory sight for visitors to Bhutan. And for good reason: perched on the face of a cliff, it encapsulates the drama and majesty of the Himalayas. It is also a site of great religious significance, as Guru Rinpoche, the founder of Buddhism in Bhutan, is said to have arrived at Taktsang on the back of a flying tiger. You won't get to ride the flying tiger, but if you are struggling with the steep hike, you may at least be able to enlist a pony ride for the ascent.

"You know, tigers are very unpredictable."

- Suraj Sharma

3

HEAR THE WORDS 'DANGPHU... DINGPHU...'

As in many parts of the world, traditional oral culture is in danger of dying out as new forms of entertainment replace storytelling. Some efforts are being taken to preserve Bhutanese folk tales, with Kunzang Choden's *Folktales of Bhutan* and Dorji Penjore's *Dangphu Dingphu* both being wonderful records of traditional stories. Bhutanese folktales traditionally begin with the words '*dangphu... dingphu...*', the meaning of which is roughly equivalent to 'a long time ago', with a longer pause between the two words signifying a greater distance between the time of the story and the present. Both collections mentioned here are available in Thimphu. Even better than reading, though, would be to hear the words '*dangphu... dingphu...*' in person...

"After nourishment, shelter and companionship, stories are the thing we need most in the world."

- Philip Pullman

4

GO IN SEARCH OF THE YETI

Known as *migoi* in Bhutan, the Yeti is the stuff of legend and folklore. Stories of the *migoi* have circulated in the region as far back as cultural memory goes: some Bon (the pre-Buddhist religion) rituals make reference to it. Of course, *migoi* don't cheerfully wander the streets of Thimphu revealing themselves to passing travelers, so catching a glimpse of the elusive creature may require leaving the beaten track, and perhaps a share of good luck or karma. Most sightings take place at altitudes of over 3,500 meters. Look out for a creature with ape-like limbs but a hairless face, exuding a foul smell, and with a hollow in its back in which it carries off its captives.

"The migoi *has powers beyond our comprehension..."*

- Kunzang Choden

5

MASTER THE BHUTANESE TOILET

As in most of Asia, and indeed the world, traditional Bhutanese toilets are of the 'squat' variety. Hard on the thighs, the position does require some coordination and a little practice to use without mishaps. The process is known to be beneficial to one's health for various reasons which need not be covered here.

Holding one's breath is also advisable.

"In awe, I watched the waxing moon ride across the zenith of the heavens like an ambered chariot towards the ebony void of infinite space wherein the tethered belts of Jupiter and Mars hang, forever festooned in their orbital majesty. And as I looked at all this I thought... I must put a roof on this toilet."

- Les Dawson

6

LEARN A MEDITATION PRACTICE

Buddha taught that the key to enlightenment is to realize the nature of one's own mind. The mind is often likened to a wild elephant, and the image opposite shows the stages of taming the mind through meditation. For this reason, meditation is the cornerstone of Buddhist practice, although in reality ritual often seems to take precedence over sitting for hours in concentration. Nevertheless, as Bhutan is the only Mahayana Buddhist country in the world, it would be a wasted opportunity to leave without learning at least one meditation practice.

"*Where is there enough leather to cover the surface of the Earth? But just having leather on the soles of one's feet is the same as covering the whole Earth. In the same way, it is not possible to control all external events; but, if I simply control my mind, what need is there to control other things?*"

- Shantideva (8th century Buddhist master)

7

FIND THE BEST MOMOS IN BHUTAN

It would be difficult to find a restaurant, bar or hotel in Bhutan that didn't offer the ubiquitous momo (steamed dumpling), as a snack or meal. Whether your preference be beef (*shakam*), pork, cheese, or veg, you have will ample chances to taste-test and compare. Of course everyone will have a different opinion as to where the best momos are served. Try them and decide for yourself.

"The only time to eat diet food is while you're waiting for the steak to cook."

- Julia Child

8

RECEIVE A PHALLUS BLESSING

We're pretty sure almost everyone reading this will already have been touched on the head by a monk wielding a wooden phallus, so this one is probably old news....

No? You've really never had a monk tap the crown of your head with an anatomically-accurate, if slightly larger than average, carved penis? Well, this is your big chance: Chimi Lakhang temple in Punakha is closely associated with the legendary Tantric master Drukpa Kunley (see #82), and it is here that you can receive such a unique blessing.

"I take refuge in the virile young tiger's Thunderbolt, rising proudly, indifferent to death."

- *Drukpa Kunley,* The Divine Madman

9

DON A GHO OR KIRA

Bhutan places great importance on its national dress. Bhutanese are required to wear it for formal occasions, when entering government buildings, and in many cases for work. Woman wear the *tego* and *kira*, a colorful silk blouse and long, straight, woven skirt respectively. Men wear the *gho*, a robe which reaches to the floor when loose, but which is hitched up to knee height and secured there with a belt. It is fiendishly difficult to put on, requiring several pairs of hands; except for the most slender and limber, even Bhutanese men often need to enlist help when dressing. Both the *gho* and *kira* come in a variety of beautiful patterns, and can be bought off the peg or tailored. We recommend dressing up at least once to do Bhutan in style!

"There are moments, Jeeves, when one asks oneself, 'Do trousers matter?'"
"The mood will pass, sir."

- P. G. Wodehouse, The Code of the Woosters

10

RIDE THE 'JUMJA SLIDE'

Most Bhutanese roads are carved out of the mountainside, horizontal strips perching precariously and improbably between vertical sheets of fragmenting rock. Yet somehow the road from Phuentsholing to Thimphu supports the heavy traffic which provides the capital, and most of the country, with its imports from India. One spot on the route, about five kilometers south of the village of Gedu, is home to a continuous landslide. The perpetual trickle, and not infrequent avalanche, of rocks has its own name: the Jumja Slide. If the road itself doesn't sound hair-raising enough, this also happens to be the spot where the cold Himalayan air meets the warm currents rising from India, resulting in the stretch being perpetually enveloped in clouds.

"It is not the clear-sighted who rule the world. Great achievements are accomplished in a blessed, warm fog."

- Joseph Conrad

11

PARTY ON IN CLOCKTOWER SQUARE

Clocktower square in Thimphu holds a variety of events and concerts. The chances are that during a visit, you may have the chance to catch either some traditional music and dancing or possibly a performance by one of the bands that form Thimphu's burgeoning rock and roll scene.

"Where words fail, music speaks."

- Hans Christian Andersen

12

HANG A PRAYER FLAG

Prayer flags are an integral part of Buddhist life in Bhutan. The colorful prayer flags are available in most general shops: buy a string of pennants and hang it between two trees or on a century-old bridge with the help of some Bhutanese children.

"Prayer does not change God, but it changes him who prays."

- Soren Kierkergaard

13

BRAVE THE RAPIDS AT PUNAKHA

The river at Punakha is divided into the Pho Chu and Mo Chu, its male and female halves respectively. They join close to Punakha Dzong, surely one of the most scenic spots in the country. Rafting trips are available, with the male half offering genuine white rapids for those seeking a bigger adrenaline rush, and the female half giving a gentler and more scenic ride.

"Row, brothers, row, the stream runs fast, the rapids are near and the daylight's past."

- Thomas Moore

14

VISIT A BHUTANESE HOME

The distinctiveness of Bhutanese houses is one of the first things that will strike visitors. Traditional houses are made from packed, or 'rammed', earth, and are solidly and spaciously built. On the bottom floor, the grain store is protected by thick walls: losing one's grain to fire in the middle of a harsh Himalayan winter would be a disaster. The attic, usually open to the air, is used for drying *emas* (chilies, green or red), as is the roof during the dry season. Bhutanese homes will also generally have a Buddhist shrine, often with a whole room dedicated to it.

"He is happiest, be he king or peasant, who finds peace in his home."

- Goethe

15

GET SNOOKERED

Depending on where you call home, this could mean to become intoxicated, to be tricked, or, in this case, to be out-foxed in a game of snooker. One of the popular leisure pastimes in Bhutan, snooker is typically, but not always, played by men. You should have no problem locating a table in a bar somewhere in Bhutan. The locals will welcome your company and while you will most likely lose the game, you will make some new friends.

"Snooker loopy nuts are we
Me and him and them and me
We'll show you what we can do
With a load of balls and a snooker cue."

- Chaz 'n' Dave, 'Snooker Loopy'

16

WATCH THE NAKED DANCERS OF SAKTENG

Perhaps the most difficult to achieve of all of the items on this list, the naked dance in remote Sakteng takes place only once every three years. The dance, known as Terchham, lasts for two days, with men between the ages of eighteen and sixty chosen to perform the dance before heading to nearby villages to receive offerings.

"I respect a man not for the clothes he wears, but for the clothes he doesn't wear. Yes, nudity is an admirable thing indeed."

- Jarod Kintz

17

FORGET ABOUT THAT AIR GUITAR AND PICK UP A DRAMNYEN

There are three main genres of Bhutanese music, each with its own sound, beauty and appeal. The oldest of these, and arguably the most 'Bhutanese', is Zhungdra. The other two are Boedra, which has Tibetan roots, and Rigzar, the modern but still uniquely Bhutanese pop music. Instruments used in all genres include the lingm (six-holed flute), the chiwang (Tibetan two-stringed fiddle), and the dramnyen which can be either three- or seven-stringed and ranges from ukulele to bass guitar size. Dramnyen are beautifully decorated and hand painted with an ornate and colorful dragon head.

"Making tools and making art define what it means to be human. Luthiers make tools for making art. It's hard to imagine a more fulfilling vocation."

- H. Luke Sandham, Master Luthier

18

FIND THE AFTER PARTY

Few people make the long and expensive trip to Bhutan specifically for the nightlife. However, it does exist, with most towns home to at least one 'dance party' (disco), as well as the ubiquitous 'cum bars' (see #43). The Bhutanese like a drink and a dance, so although the bars and clubs close a little early (the clubs shut at 1am in Thimphu although you might find yourself granted an extra hour on public holidays), there is usually something going on after the official closing time. In fact, some of the after-hours spots are rather surprising (see #27!). As a result of the attentions of the police, the location of the after party does tend to shift with the swirling winds of karma: to find it, we can only suggest that you make friends and ask around.

"What hath night to do with sleep?"

- Milton, Paradise Lost

19

MEET A YAK AND LEARN ITS NAME

Yaks are herded at higher altitudes, and while hiking you may stumble across a yak herder's hut in a meadow or even find yourself nose to nose with a yak on the trail. A famous *lozey* (see #37) tells of a yak's sorrow at having to depart its herd for the slaughterhouse, a lament which sums up the hard life that these beasts of burden live. To alleviate the sorrow, try to befriend a yak: perhaps the herder can tell you its name.

"Until one has loved an animal a part of one's soul remains unawakened."

- Anatole France

20

CROSS INTO INDIA

The border crossing into India at Phuentsholing is always busy with streams of traders moving back and forth, but is not generally on visitors' itineraries. The Indian check point is set back a few hundred meters from the gate, so if you ask the Bhutanese border officers nicely, you may be able to cross into India: the noise and chaos will immediately tell you that you are no longer in Bhutan. Once in Jaigaon, the town on the Indian side, you can explore the shopping district, have lunch, and take your photo with a cow in the street, before returning to Bhutan.

"Beyond that border I don't belong."

- J. D. Souther, 'The Border Guard'

21

COUNT THE CHORTENS AT DOCHU-LA

Many visitors to Bhutan traverse the Dochu-la pass as it lies between the Thimphu and Punakha valleys. The 108 chortens (are there really exactly 108?) at the peak were commissioned by the eldest of the four Queen Mothers to commemorate the casualties in the 2003 border conflict in southern Bhutan, a war in which the Fourth King served on the front lines. On a clear day, the view from the chortens of the crystalline mountain peaks on the Tibetan border is simply spectacular.

"Nobody climbs mountains for scientific reasons. Science is used to raise money for the expeditions, but you really climb for the hell of it."

- Edmund Hillary

22

NO BREECHES, NO BLOUSE: NO BLESSINGS

Don't waste a trip to a monastery only to be denied entrance. Buddhist etiquette requires visitors to dress modestly with covered shoulders and legs while visiting holy places such as monasteries and shrines.

"I believe in God, but not as one thing, not as an old man in the sky. I believe that what people call God is something in all of us. I believe that what Jesus and Mohammed and Buddha and all the rest said was right. It's just that the translations have gone wrong."

- John Lennon

23

MAIL YOURSELF HOME

Since first being printed in the 1960s, Bhutanese postage stamps have become known for their variety, beauty, and innovative designs. These include the world's first 3D stamp, bas-relief and sculptural stamps, stamps printed on silk or steel foil, scented rose stamps, and the famous Talking Stamps, miniature records which could be played on a normal record player. Go to the main post office in Thimphu and mingle with the collectors viewing the hundreds of different stamps on offer there. And if you want to give your folks at home a surprise, take a flash drive with a picture of yourself, (or anything else!) and they will print legally accepted Bhutanese postage stamps for you with your images on them.

"I love the rebelliousness of snail mail, and I love anything that can arrive with a postage stamp. There's something about that person's breath and hands on the letter."

- Diane Lane

24

SPOT ALL EIGHT OF THE AUSPICIOUS SYMBOLS

The eight auspicious symbols possess great significance in Himalayan Buddhism. If you don't know what they are – and few do – you can ask anyone… or you can cheat and look at the bottom of the page. Hint: You will frequently see them painted on buildings and homes.

They are: the conch, the precious umbrella, the victory banner, the golden fish, the dharma wheel, the endless knot, the lotus flower and the treasure vase.

25

DO THE BULL'S EYE DANCE

Archery is the national sport of Bhutan. It is usually more of a social experience than a highly competitive sport, with a great deal of teasing and ribbing taking place between teams. When an archer hits the bull's eye, he and his team do the dance. Ask to join in, do your best, take it semi-seriously, and you'll be welcomed: it's only around twenty seconds long. However, consider long and hard if you are offered a chance to participate in the archery as it would be a shame for an inexpert archer to hit a bystander.

"It's all fun and games until someone loses an eye and then all the 'I'm sorry's' in the world won't bring back that eye."

- Suzie Henthorn, Professional Downhill Skier

26

EAT YOUR VEGETABLES

Ema datsi, the national dish of Bhutan, is eaten for nearly every meal, morning, noon and night. *Emas* (chilies) range from red hot to white hot, and are eaten raw, cooked, deep-fried, with or without rice, but mostly made into a stew with the tangy local cheese. For each day you are in Bhutan, you will have at least one, and more likely two or three, chances to enjoy this dish, and therefore plentiful opportunities for imaginative descriptions of the experience. Your first three days are provided free of charge on the next page.

1. Like putting your tongue on the tailpipe of a Harley Davidson after a long ride;

2. Like the hood of a black hearse in Death Valley on the Fourth of July;

3. Like drinking napalm with your morning coffee.

Just try some and you'll find inspiration … there's a special prize for anyone who makes it to a baker's dozen!

"A little gasoline... blowtorch... no problem."

- Delia, **Beetlejuice**

27

VISIT BUDDHA POINT

No visit to Bhutan is complete without experiencing both the Buddha himself and the panoramic views of Thimphu that he enjoys. The huge golden Buddha is known to catch sunlight even when the surrounding areas lie in shadow. Buddha point is still under construction, but nevertheless offers great photo opportunities by day, a gathering place for young Bhutanese after dark, and great views in several directions at all times. Visit by day, or evening, or both!

"The world is full of magic things, patiently waiting for our senses to grow sharper."

- W.B. Yeats

28

LEARN YOUR 'KS'

Since Bhutan was unified over a century ago, the Wangchuk Dynasty has ruled over the country. They did so as an absolute monarchy until 2008, when the Fourth King abdicated, handing power to his son, but at the same time instituting a democratic system. The kings inspire great respect and love in their subjects, and are known affectionately as K1-K5. The reign of each had its own characteristics: making an effort to learn what each is known for will enrich your understanding of the country and its political system.

"Throughout my reign I will never rule you as a King. I will protect you as a parent, care for you as a brother and serve you as a son. I shall give you everything and keep nothing."

- H.M. King Jigme Khesar Namgyel Wangchuk

29

DO BATTLE WITH THE LEECHES OF GEDU

While increased population and cultivation have resulted in reducing the leech presence, there are still many places in the clouds where the dampness and mild temperatures during the monsoon season mean plentiful leeches. The town of Gedu, about an hour north of Pheuntsholing, is home to the Royal University of Bhutan College of Business Studies, an unpredictable climate, and a whole lot of leeches. Remember that the worst part is thinking about them: leech bites are actually painless, and you can give a leech a chance to live for up to a year by providing it with one small meal.

"When I woke up this morning, leeches were crawling up my thighs. The little vampires go undetected: before they feast they anesthetize."

- D. L. Sloan, 'Leech Season in Bhutan'

30

CALCULATE THE PUNCH OF A BOTTLE OF BHUTANESE BEER

There are several iterations of local beer, mostly of the Druk brand, with the notable exception of the tasty but unfiltered Red Panda from Bumthang. By far the best-selling brand, however, is Druk. Three varieties are available: Lager, Supreme and the original 11,000. The latter proclaims its strength as 'not less than 9%', and at 650ml per bottle, you'll know all about it the morning after. If your throbbing head is able to handle it, try calculate how many cans of Bud Light would pack the same punch as a single bottle of 11,000.

"You can't be a real country unless you have a beer and an airline."

- Frank Zappa

31

FIND THE STATUE OF 1000-ARMED AVALOKITESHVARA

Sangchhen Dorji Lhendrup nunnery, perched on the shoulder of a hill a short drive from the town of Kuruthang in Punakha, offers panoramic views in both directions along the valley. However, the real treasure to be found here is the statue of Avalokiteshvara, the Buddha of compassion (also known as Chenrezig). In general, Buddhist deities can take a number of forms; Avalokiteshvara has a thousand arms and numerous heads in order to better help sentient beings escape from the cycle of suffering known as 'samsara'. You may have to ask a caretaker to unlock the central temple, but the statue is spectacular. If you are lucky, you may even catch a ceremony in progress.

"Avalokiteshvara Bodhisattva is the Hearer of the Cries of the World."

- John Daido Loori

32

PLAY BADMINTON WITH MONKS

The monks in Bhutan spend a great deal of their time in meditation, study, and taking part in ceremonies. However, they are permitted some recreation, and often enjoy batting a shuttlecock back and forth, kicking a soccer ball around, or even a game of volleyball. If you can find a game, you'll be very welcome to join in.

"There's sketch, improv, writing, acting, music, and badminton. Those are the seven forms of comedy."

- T. J. Miller

33

MAKE A FRIEND AND STAY IN TOUCH

The Bhutanese are friendly in general, if not particularly outgoing. They do tend to be curious about foreigners, particularly outside the capital. There are plenty of opportunities to strike up a conversation: you might find yourself approached without doing anything much, but shared taxis, bus rides, and chit chat as do your shopping are also chances to exchange pleasantries with locals. Taking time to form a friendship with a Bhutanese will give you a real insight into how life is lived here, as well as a sense of the accepting and tolerant attitude that gave birth to the concept of Gross National Happiness. Most Bhutanese are fairly tech-savvy and are keen users of social media, so a chance meeting may turn into a lifelong friendship.

"We were together, I forget the rest."

- Walt Whitman

34

THE BIRDS. THE BIRDS.

Thanks to its varied elevation, Bhutan is home to an extraordinary biodiversity. That, and a strategic location on one of the major Asian migratory flight pathways, makes Bhutan a dream destination for serious birders. There are many rare – and sometimes unique – birds that can be seen throughout the year, one of the most famous species of which is the black-necked crane. The bird migrates from Tibet, and settles in Bumthang valley in the winter, between late October and mid-February. As such, it is an elusive sight, but one worth making the effort to catch. Bhutan is also home to a number of endangered species which will hopefully be given a chance to thrive thanks to the country's extensive national parks and system of protected areas. Endangered species include – and we aren't making these up – the blackish-breasted babbler; the white-rumped vulture; the ferruginous duck, the satyr tragopan; and a nice one to finish with: the beautiful nuthatch.

"The eagle flies with the dove, if you can't be with the one you love.... love the one you're with."

Stephen Stills, 'Love the One You're With'

35

EXPLORE A ROADSIDE CAVE

You will see a number of small caves as you drive from town to town in Bhutan. Many of these house numerous tiny chortens – the tapered pillars which represent the mind of Buddha – which are left as offerings. Take a few minutes out to climb into a cave temple and enjoy a few moments of peace.

"There are many things worth living for, a few things worth dying for, and nothing worth killing for."

- *Tom Robbins, author of* Another Roadside Attraction

36

GET TEASED BY ATSARA

During festivals, known as *tshechus*, it is possible to watch a variety of traditional religious and secular dances. However, many would argue that the real stars of the show are not the dancers, but the jesters, known as Atsara. Wearing distinctive red masks, they have license to improvise, tease, and indulge in general clowning. Even the dancers are not exempted from their attentions, so if you're feeling brave, find yourself a spot near the front. Be warned, though: we have seen a phallus-wielding Atsara charge at full-tilt towards a shrieking girl…

"Jesters do oft prove prophets."

- William Shakespeare

37

FOLLOW IN THE FOOTSTEPS OF PEMI TSHEWANG TASHI

The *lozey* is a traditional ballad form, recited with a distinctive staccato rhythm. *The Ballad of Pemi Tshewang Tashi* is one of only a handful of *lozey* to have been translated into English. The ballad tells of how Chamberlain Pemi Tshewang Tashi is unwillingly sent to war during the civil strife in nineteenth century Bhutan, and describes his journey eastwards towards Trongsa, where his forces are defeated. While it would be difficult to follow Pemi Tshewang Tashi's exact route – it would be a journey on foot taking several days – the dramatic cliff at Trongsa Dzong is still as it was when the Chamberlain met his death.

"The command of Zongpon Angdruk Nim-
To dismiss it, as dear as gold,
To carry it out, is heavy as the hills."

- *Karma Ura,* The Ballad of Pemi Tshewang Tashi

38

ENJOY A LUNCH BOX AT DRUKGYEL DZONG

The perfect spot for a picnic, the ruined Drukgyel Dzong is several miles past the frequently visited Tiger's Nest (#2) in Paro valley. It has great historical significance, being the point at which the Bhutanese held off invading Tibetan forces in the seventeenth century, the only time Bhutan has ever been invaded. Although it sadly suffered the fate of several other *dzongs* and monasteries when it burnt down in the 1950s, the ruins have their own drama as well as spectacular views of the lush Paro valley to the south and more forbidding crags and Mount Jumolhari visible to the north.

"*Ruins pose a direct challenge to our concern with power and rank, with bustle and fame. They puncture the inflated folly of our exhaustive and frenetic pursuit of wealth.*"

- *Alain de Botton*

39

JOIN IN A SINGALONG

The Bhutanese tend to be quite musical, and a night with friends at someone's house will often turn into an impromptu singalong. If you are able to make a Bhutanese friend (see #33), you may be lucky enough to find yourself at a party: sit back, relax, and enjoy the hospitality and the music. Be prepared to have the guitar handed to you so you can take your turn. Everyone in Bhutan can play and sing a tune or two, so if you say that you can't strum, or even hum, no one will believe you… so it is best to come prepared with at least one party piece up your sleeve.

"If more of us valued food and cheer and song above hoarded gold, it would be a merrier world."

- Thorin Oakenshield, The Hobbit

40

ATTEND A PUJA

Buddhist religious ceremonies, collectively known as 'pujas', are common sights and sounds in Bhutan. Each household will invite a lama and his attendant monks once a year to bless the house, with friends and relatives also invited for a feast. Surefire signs that a puja is taking place are the distinctive sounds of the monks' horns – you might mistake the noise for the pained lowing of a cow – and the acrid smell of smoke as offerings are burnt. If you put your head in the door and look curious, the chances are that you will be invited to partake of the food and drink provided by the host family, and to sit and watch (probably in total incomprehension!) as the rituals are performed.

"Thousands of candles can be lighted from a single candle, and the life of the candle will not be shortened. Happiness never decreases by being shared."

- Buddha

41

DISCOVER A TERMA

While Guru Rinpoche brought Buddhism to Bhutan, he sought to preserve his teachings by concealing sacred texts and treasures, known as *termas*, around the country. Enlightened treasure finders, known as *tertons*, would then be able to recover these artefacts. Gom Kora, between Trashigang and Tashi Yangtse, is home to an imprint of the guru's foot, a phallus-shaped rock belonging to the great *terton* Pema Lingpa, and, if you're feeling particularly meritorious, a sin-testing alleyway.

"Memory is the treasure house of the mind wherein the monuments thereof are kept and preserved."

- Thomas Fuller

42

A BIRD'S EYE VIEW OF EVEREST

While the world's highest peak is some distance from Bhutan in western Himalayas, many flight routes into Paro afford an excellent view of Everest as it thrusts through the cloud cover. The captain often makes an announcement when Everest comes into view, but keep your eyes peeled anyway: it's pretty much unmissable! The best view of Everest, however, is on the short flight between Paro and Kathmandu, which is surely one of the most spectacular in the world as the plane skirts along the southern edge of the Greater Himalayan Range.

"The first question which you will ask and which I must try to answer is this: What is the use of climbing Mount Everest? And my answer must at once be, it is no use. There is not the slightest prospect of any gain whatsoever."

- George Leigh Mallory

43

DRINK IN A 'CUM BAR'

The Latin 'cum', meaning 'with', has worked its way into Bhutanese English. As such, you will see many establishments announcing themselves as 'restaurant cum bar', 'grocery cum restaurant' or similar. Unfortunately, the grammar does not always survive completely intact, leading to some places advertising themselves simply as 'cum bar'. These traditional, 'hole-in-the-wall' joints are well worth a visit, however, and are an authentic way to sample a bottle or two of Druk 11000 (see #30).

"The sway of alcohol over mankind is unquestionably due to its power to stimulate the mystical faculties of human nature, usually crushed to earth by the cold facts and dry criticisms of the sober hour."

- William James

44

LEARN THE DIFFERENCE BETWEEN DAY AND NIGHT HUNTING

Suffice to say that there is no traditional culture of day hunting in Bhutan…

"Courtship consists in a number of quiet attentions, not so pointed as to alarm, nor so vague as not to be understood."

- Laurence Sterne

45

NAME THE ANIMALS THAT MAKE UP THE TAKIN

The takin, national animal of Bhutan, is unusual in appearance. According to Bhutanese folklore, they are a combination of three animals: we will leave it to you to guess what these are once you have seen a takin in the flesh. Classified as 'vulnerable' by the International Union for Conservation of Nature, the easiest way to see them is in the Takin Reserve in the Motithang district of Thimphu. The fourth king experimented with releasing them from captivity in the 1980s, but after causing several weeks of chaos on the streets of the capital, they were rounded up and returned to the safety of the reserve.

"The greatness of a nation and its moral progress can be judged by the way its animals are treated."

- Mahatma Gandhi

46

STRUT YOUR STUFF IN A DRAYANG

A little like karaoke, but with dancing. And without the bad singing. With female dancers and quite often musicians, so sort of like a strip club, but without a pole. And no stripping. In fact, the entertainers are dressed from neck to ankle to wrist in traditional attire and stay that way. Considered 'racy' by Bhutanese standards, drayang bars are mostly frequented my men who tip talented young women to sing songs and perform traditional Bhutanese dances. The singing and dancing is generally of high quality and good entertainment. If it wasn't a late night activity you really could bring the kids. And if you happen to imbibe of the *ara*, (see #62) you may find yourself on stage with a microphone, showing off your moves.

"If you can sit happy with embarrassment, there's not much else that can really get to ya."

- Christian Bale

47

COUNT THE WATERFALLS ON THE ROAD TO PHEUNTSHOLING

Bhutan's mountainous terrain makes it home to countless spectacular waterfalls. The drive south from Chukkha towards Pheuntsholing, in particular, is fantastic for waterfall spotting: you will see waterfalls of all sizes from spectacular torrents tumbling hundreds of meters down the hillsides to numerous smaller cascades. Each beautiful in its own right. Depending on the season, you can probably stop counting after a few dozen.

"I beg your pardon, Owl, but I th-th-th-think we coming to a fatterfall... a flutterfall... a very big waterfall!"

- *Piglet,* Winnie the Pooh

48

CIRCUMAMBULATE AND SPIN

There are many large and beautifully decorated prayer wheels in Bhutan. You can't miss the one in Paro town square but they are all over Bhutan, sometimes where you least expect to find them. You will find Bhutanese of all ages walking clockwise around the prayer wheels and spinning them at all times of day and night. Take a spin yourself: it will give you a good moment to reflect, and will result in the ringing of the bell.

"The prayer wheel is about bringing peace and harmony in our global community."

- Tenzin Dhonden

49

WATCH A BHUTANESE MOVIE

Bhutan is home to a small but vibrant film industry. The government subsidizes and encourages film-making as a way to preserve the national culture and language. Some movies do have English subtitles which will allow you to follow the action, but otherwise sit back and enjoy the very Bhutanese scenery, music, dancing and melodrama. The easiest place to catch a movie is the theatre located upstairs in Thimphu's City Mall.

Dondup: I'm going very, very far away. To the land of my dreams. That's where I'm going.
The Monk: To a dreamland? You should be careful with dreamlands. Because... when you wake up, it may not be very pleasant.

- Travelers and Magicians

50

CHEW YOUR WAY THROUGH A WHOLE LUMP OF DOMA

Also known as beetelnut or paan, and rarely a treat for the uninitiated, *doma* an essential part of the day for many, many people in Bhutan. The resultant red lips, gums and tongue are what gives that vampire look. The face most people pull when chewing *doma* for the first time suggests that it would be unlikely to catch on, but the practice dates back several centuries and is widespread. See if you can stick with it, at least long enough to spit out the red juice, which will invariably splash onto your own shoes.

"I learned early to drink beer, wine and whiskey. And I think I was about five when I first chewed tobacco."

- Babe Ruth

51

TAKE A SELFIE IN A THICKET OF 'PIG FOOD'

Known locally as '*maal*', and as 'hemp' most places, it grows prolifically at certain elevations and seasonally in Bhutan. Traditionally used as forage for pigs (presumably because it made them agreeable, lazy and hungry), it is not suitable for recreational purposes due to very low THC content. However, it is useful for preventing erosion around rice paddies, and for interesting photo opportunities. At different times throughout the year entire mountainsides are covered with brilliant green fern-like hemp.

"Herb is the healing of a nation, alcohol is the destruction."

- Bob Marley

52

PARLOUR GAMES AND TEA

For 'parlour', read 'back street' or 'dingy cum-bar' and for tea, read 'Druk 11000'. Two games at the more rugged end of Bhutanese life, and played on the street or in shop doorways, are *Karom* and *Parala*. *Karom* is a variant on shuffleboard while *Parala* – or *Yam* – involves dice and money, is technically illegal, but is still fairly widely played. Games seem to last all day and groups of players can sit clustered round the game for whole weekends. We're at a loss as to the arcane rules of both, but as always in Bhutan, locals are generally willing to help out a confused guest.

"Games lubricate the mind and the body."

- Benjamin Franklin

53

LEARN THE EARTH-RAMMING SONG

While most new homes in Bhutan are now made of concrete, the traditional means of construction was, and remains, rammed earth. If properly maintained, rammed earth homes with a slate roof will last indefinitely, or at least until an inauspicious event makes it necessary to vacate the structure and build a new one nearby. This method of construction is labor-intensive but eco-friendly, and the whole village helps out by pounding the earth into frames for days at a time as the walls rise inch by inch. To pass the time, the men and women tease each other, with the menfolk liable to have their masculinity called into questions if it is felt that their tamping zeal is flagging. The real motivator, though, is the song 'Om Sangla Mani'. Sung to help the rammers keep rhythm and to lift spirits, it also conveys blessings on the building as it is built. It may very well be the most beautiful sound you'll ever hear. And of course if you have the opportunity to join in, all the better as many hands make light work.

"Whistle while you work ... when hearts are high the time will fly, so whistle while you work."

- From Snow White and the Seven Dwarfs

54

WALK ACROSS ONE OF THE IRON MONK'S BRIDGES

Thangtong Gyalpo, known as the Iron Monk, brought ironworking technology to Bhutan in the 15th century and built several suspension bridges in the country. Some have been rebuilt and preserved. If you can find one and walk across it, you will earn merit and good luck. It will also make your heart pound as the walking area is typically made of loose wire mesh and is very transparent. Don't look down... keep your eyes focused on the far side, and march!

"Like a bridge over troubled water, I will ease your mind."

- Paul Simon

55

LEARN THE FOUR NOBLE TRUTHS

Buddhism is central to life in Bhutan, with its ubiquitous iconography a very visible reminder of this fact. This art is not simply decorative, however, and its rich symbolism reflects the Buddhist view of the world. Some understanding of Buddhism will therefore enhance your appreciation of art in the country as well as the values that people aspire to live by. We suggest you begin with the Four Noble Truths, Buddha's first teaching following his enlightenment. The four truths are: true sufferings, true origins, true cessations and true paths. Achieving #71 on the list may give you more insight.

"Now this, bhikkhus, is the noble truth of suffering: birth is suffering, aging is suffering, illness is suffering, death is suffering; union with what is displeasing is suffering; separation from what is pleasing is suffering; not to get what one wants is suffering..."

- Buddha

56

COUNT THE TONGUES

Bhutan is linguistically very diverse. Younger Bhutanese will speak English as it has been the medium of instruction in schools since the 1960s. All will speak Dzongkha, the national language; others, especially those from southern Bhutan, will possibly speak Nepali; those hailing from the east will prefer to speak Sharchop, while those from the middle of the country may speak Bumthangkha, or another of the nearly two dozen distinct languages of Bhutan. If you are going to choose one of these, Dzongkha is a good bet. Mastering 'hello', 'thank you' and 'I love Bhutan', will earn you instant popularity. When at a gathering with three or more Bhutanese, try to find out what languages each speaks: the current record at a single dinner is over a dozen!

"The more elaborate our means of communication, the less we communicate."

- Joseph Priestly

57

GRAB A BARGAIN IN THE CENTENNIAL MARKET

The Centennial Market is the main shopping place for fruits, grains and vegetables in the capital. Local seasonal produce will usually be found on the upper level, with imported foods on the ground level. Highlights include the dried fish area, after which you will appreciate a timely visit to the locally-made incense area.

"Whoever said money can't buy happiness simply didn't know where to go shopping."

- Bo Derek

58

VISIT PARO DZONG – AND MORE

The Paro Dzong is a part of almost every visit to Bhutan, but nearby are some less well-known surprises. From Paro town one must cross the Paro Chu (Paro River), via the centuries old cantilever bridge, to reach the *dzong*. If possible, go in March when thousands of Bhutanese and a few hundred tourists make this pilgrimage to attend the Paro *tshechu* (the ten day long religious festival). The Parops – people from the fertile and hence wealthy Paro valley – have a reputation for wearing the flashiest *ghos* and *kiras*, so in addition to the majestic *dzong*, the people themselves are a sight to behold.

However, don't let your experience of Paro end there…

"You have a more interesting life if you wear impressive clothes."

- Vivienne Westwood

59

FIND THE BLUE ROCK

… after crossing the bridge and ticking off #58, retrace your footsteps, and instead of progressing up the path to the *dzong*, turn right and follow the path in a southerly direction along the river bank. Less than a hundred meters below the bridge, you will find a very large, bright blue rock covered in various painted bas relief images as well as quotes of Buddha and Bhutanese Buddhist saints. This impressive site is maintained by students from the nearby College of Education and is rarely visited by foreigners.

As unusual as the rock is, we still aren't quite done with Paro…

"Two roads diverged in a wood, and I - I took the one less traveled by, and that has made all the difference."

- Robert Frost

60

RECEIVE A BLESSING IN THE SHADOW OF THE DZONG

After you've seen Paro Dzong (#58) and the blue rock (#59), walk back upstream along the narrow path by the river. After a hundred meters, right at the water line and connected to the river, you will find a tiny and rarely visited shrine cut out of the stone riverbank. Here, in the shadow of the ancient *dzong* that towers above, you may get a blessing from the attendant monk. Due to the very conservative nature of the monks that attend and maintain this shrine visitors are not allowed to enter, but are welcome to visit and seek blessings.

"Sometimes the road less traveled is less traveled for a reason."

- Jerry Seinfeld

61

FIND A CAT

Visitors to Bhutan are usually struck by the number of street dogs. They are not generally aggressive towards people, being more preoccupied with intra-dog gang warfare and getting fed. They also tend to sleep on main roads and intersections with remarkable insouciance. However, the question is this: with so many dogs ruling the roost, can you take up the challenge to find a Bhutanese cat?

"In times of joy, all of us wished we possessed a tail we could wag."

- W.H. Auden

62

TASTE-TEST THE ARA

Collect a minimum of three bottles of *ara*, the traditional and locally brewed liquor of Bhutan. Brewed in homes, no two batches taste alike. Blind taste-test your collection with friends, new or old, and rate each brew on smoothness, finish, palate, legs, clarity, and punch! As a suggestion, it is considered prudent to drink *ara* only when the maker is known to the drinker or at least known to a second party: bad *ara* can be very, very bad.

"Candy is dandy but liquor is quicker."

- Ogden Nash

63

LEARN A MANTRA

The word 'mantra' (along with the word 'guru') was not invented by writers of best-selling business books. Mantra is an ancient term referring to a sacred utterance possessing spiritual power. In Buddhism, mantras are often associated with particular Buddhas, who themselves embody particular qualities such as compassion, wisdom, or power. If you come across a muttering Bhutanese, they are more likely to be reciting a mantra than cursing under their breath. Find someone to teach you a mantra: it will provide you with a practice and source of comfort for the rest of your life.

"Om mani padme hum"

- the mantra of Avalokiteshvara, the Buddha of compassion.

64

WATCH A WEAVER AT WORK

The *kiras* and *ghos* which comprise Bhutanese national dress are traditionally hand-woven, usually by women. Some of the more elaborate designs take a great deal of time and skill to weave. They are also expensive, with a festival *kira* costing as much as 120,000 Ngultrum (close to $2,000), but it is telling of the great importance that the Bhutanese attach to these fabrics that they are willing, despite low average incomes, to pay for them. The eastern district of Lhuntse is particularly well-known for its weavers, but if you are unable to make it that far, you should still be able to catch a weaver in action either in Thimphu at the National Textile Museum or in Paro at the weaving shop near the playground.

"We all have our own life to pursue, our own dream to be weaving."

- Louisa May Alcott

65

DISCOVER THE LITERATURE OF THE MOUNTAINS

The Mountain Echoes literary festival is held in Thimphu every spring. It attracts a number of interesting figures from Bhutan and beyond: previous guests have included Bollywood actresses, adventurers to Antarctica, filmmakers, translators of Indian epics, and tellers of folktales. The events are open to the public and are free of charge. Of particular interest to visitors is the small body of Bhutanese literature, written in English by Bhutanese writers, and not readily available outside Bhutan. Junction Bookstore near the main traffic circle in Thimphu is a good place to find out about the country's literature.

"Literature is the art of discovering something extraordinary about ordinary people, and saying with ordinary words something extraordinary."

- Boris Pasternak

66

PLAY KHURU WITHOUT INJURING YOURSELF OR OTHERS

Khuru, like archery, is a popular sport involving sharp objects launched at high speed over considerable distances with a high level of skill. And often involving some drinking. Think Jarts, the lawn dart game popular in the 1980s, but on steroids. The *khuru* resembles an oversized dart, with experienced players able to impart spin onto it in order to keep its trajectory steady. The target is small, placed on the ground, and is extremely difficult to hit, or even to even get close to, for beginners. You might see a game in progress and ask to join in; otherwise, there are often *khuru* stalls set up at festivals where you will be able to play for a small fee.

"You can get the dart player out of the pub, but you can't get the pub out of the dart player."

- Sid Waddell

67

TAKE A SHARED TAXI

The main ways that Bhutanese get around the country are by bus or shared taxi. Both are social ways to travel, but the latter are a little more comfortable. A shared taxi stand can be found in every town and at many crossroads, and is usually fairly obvious as the drivers stand next to their vehicles shouting their destinations. The rate is fixed, so is generally divided by four (one passenger in the front and three in the back), although it is possible to simply have the car to yourself – this is usually referred to as 'reserve' – or to agree between two or three of you to split the cost if you don't want to wait for the car to fill up before departing.

"Happiness is like a kiss. You must share it to enjoy it."

- Bernard Meltzer

68

FIND THE TOWN IN THE PHALLUS ANECDOTE

Many houses in Bhutan have colorful murals painted on the exterior walls. One of the common murals is an alert phallus. A story goes that two young men were traveling in Bhutan some years ago. Upon seeing such a mural, one of the men was heard to say to the other: "They painted your portrait on the side of the house!" His friend replied, "Oh yeah? Well, they named a town after you!" What was the name of the town he was referring to? (Hint: It's near Chukkha on the national highway).

"It is one of the severest tests of friendship to tell your friend his faults. So to love a man that you cannot bear to see a stain upon him, and to speak painful truth through loving words, that is friendship."

- Henry Ward Beecher

69

FIND YOUR OWN MONASTERY

There are countless monasteries in Bhutan, some requiring vigorous trekking to reach, and some more easily accessible. Choose one or more to visit based on your own timetable, energy level, and fitness. Remote monasteries tend to receive few visitors, so dropping in on the monks there (and dropping off some vegetables or rice), will provide an unusual and memorable experience. The more remote, the more special the experience is likely to be, and more effort expended means more merit earned!

"My imagination is a monastery and I am its monk."

- John Keats

70

LEARN A TRADITIONAL DANCE

Traditional dancing is a large part of life in Bhutan. All Bhutanese school children learn to dance (and sing) from an early age. The steps are not difficult and are reminiscent of a Hawaiian hula, (including the graceful hand movements), crossed with country and western line dancing. Even the least rhythmically gifted should be able to give it a try without embarrassing themselves unduly.

"I don't know but I've been told: if you keep on dancing you'll never grow old."

- Steve Miller

71

CHAT WITH A MONK

There are many monks in Bhutan and you will encounter them frequently wherever you go. Most will welcome a few minutes of conversation with you. Don't be shy, smile and converse: you may receive some useful spiritual advice, or simply some interesting insights into monastery life.

"My idea of good company is the company of clever, well-informed people who have a great deal of conversation; that is what I call good company."

- Jane Austen

72

HITCH A RIDE

In much of the world, the golden days of hitchhiking are sadly a thing of the past, largely due to suspicion and perceived danger. However, Bhutan is a country where motor vehicles are still a fairly new phenomenon, and in which community spirit and generosity towards strangers are very strong. As such, hitching a ride is still a common way of getting around for locals, and the Bhutanese will generally offer a ride to foreigners. They also tend to be remarkably willing to go out of their way to take you to your destination. So don't be shy, stick out your arm, and see who picks you up.

"I will hail them, my brothers of the wheel, and pitch them a yarn, of the sort that has been so successful hitherto; and they will give me a lift, of course..."

- Mr. Toad, The Wind in the Willows

73

GO EYE-TO-EYE WITH A BULL

The term 'cowboy' in Bhutan refers to a fellow running a herd of as many as six cows and a bull. Normally oblivious to vehicles large and small, bulls are known to express interest in two wheelers, whether to mate or from jealousy is unknown. Typically allowed to roam free, they are rarely aggressive unless provoked. But don't push your luck, and watch out for 'the look' that bulls give when evaluating you as alien, girlfriend or rival!

"No rancher has the right to sell, or own, what God meant to be free. The Range must always remain open."

- BBQ Bill Shankelbean

74

RED RED RICE

According to a vendor at Centennial Market, (see #57), the original title of the UB40 hit single was inspired by the red rice of Paro. He claims it was later changed to 'wine' for broader appeal to western audiences. Regardless of the veracity or otherwise of this tale, the red rice is tastier than its white counterpart, and helps to dull the fire of the chilies in most Bhutanese dishes. If you want to see where this rice is grown, take a walk across the floor of the lovely Paro valley. One of the most fertile and prosperous agricultural areas of Bhutan, it is carpeted with rice paddies that become an almost luminous green during the spring and summer months. Separating each paddy is a narrow dyke which also serves as a foot path to allow farmers to traverse the fields.

"Red is the ultimate cure for sadness."

- Bill Blass

75

TOUCH THE CLOUDS

For much of the year, Bhutan has crystal clear skies. This is a wonderful thing, as there is nothing quite like watching colorful prayer flags fluttering against the azure of the sky and the green of the mountains. However, around the wetter summer months, the clouds often descend tantalizingly low, with fronds of white spreading along the hillsides almost, it seems, within touching distance. Walking a couple of hundred meters upwards will often take you into the mists themselves, a border state between the valleys below and the muted grey world of the rocks at your feet. Continue on, and within minutes you may find clear blue skies above you, and a view of nothing but the billowing white clouds below you. Such is the vertical nature of the topography of Bhutan.

"For I have danced the streets of heaven,
And touched the face of God."

- Cuthbert Hicks

76

WAIT OUT AN ELEPHANT DELAY

Bhutan is constitutionally committed to preserving not less than 65% of land mass as forest. Due to wide variations in elevation, the relatively small land area of Bhutan is home to an immense variety of flora and fauna. Along the rarely-visited reaches of the southern border, wild elephants roam back and forth across the Indian border without visas or passports. West Bengalese frequently complain about delays in rail transport caused by Bhutanese elephants crossing or standing on the tracks.

"God is really only another artist. He invented the giraffe, the elephant, and the cat. He has no real style. He just keeps on trying other things."

- Charlie Chaplin

77

FIND THE OTHER ELEPHANT

This is a different type of elephant to #76. To the sharp-eyed, a life-size elephant is visible in a natural rock formation. It is close to the Chuzom junction, 'chu' meaning 'river', and 'sum' meaning 'three'. So, from the three rivers confluence, head towards Thimphu, and look up on sharp curves. Please don't do this activity while driving!

"Loyalty was a great thing, but no lieutenants should be forced to choose between their leader and a circus with elephants."

- Neil Gaiman, **Good Omens: The Nice and Accurate Prophecies of Agnes Nutter, Witch**

78

DONATE YOUR AIRPORT BOOK

Take time out to visit the tiny public library on Norzim Lam in Thimphu. Try to donate a book or two if you have any with you, and consider buying an unusual book from the 'For Sale' pile. The prices are reasonable and you'll likely end up with a decades-old book that you never would have seen or acquired elsewhere.

"I've never understood the notion of boredom. As human beings we have not only our imaginations, memories, and knowledge, but importantly we have access to the imaginations, memories and knowledge of others. We have books. If you feel you are in danger of becoming bored, simply pick up a book."

- P. J. Kavanagh

79

RESPECT THE CURRENCY

Each denomination of Bhutanese currency bears an image of one of the five Kings. To avoid disrespect, do not crumple, destroy or deface the currency.

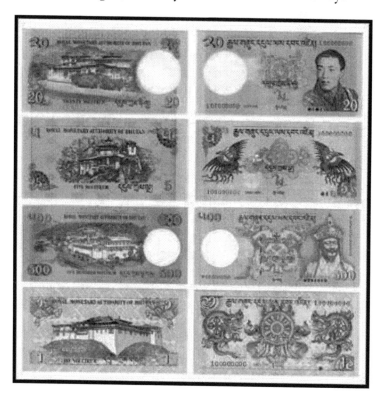

"Cash is cash. Everything else is not cash."

- Ugyen Tenzin

80

ALLOW FOR THE UNEXPECTED

Bhutan's unique approach to tourism means that visitors are required to have a fixed itinerary. However, this does not mean that a trip can't accommodate the unexpected, and some of Bhutan's finest moments arise through spontaneity. An impromptu gathering, unannounced holiday (these happen frequently), a delay in scheduled transportation caused by a rockslide (these also happen frequently), an astonishing view just round the corner (these happen continuously), can result in a flash of insight into a different way of life. All can be found by deviating a little from the script.

"And what exactly, may I ask, were you expecting?"

- Tenzin Lodr

81

TAKE A HOT STONE BATH

The hot springs at Gasa, several hours' rough drive north of Punakha, are said to have medicinal qualities. Many Bhutanese make the long trip there for this purpose, but for others the next best thing is a hot stone bath. A traditional form of relaxation in Bhutan, the bath itself is actually made of wood. Stones are heated on an open fire, then placed in a separate compartment of the bath, with much steam and sizzling, to heat the water. Many tourist hotels now offer stone baths, but for the real experience find an outdoor bath: sometimes these are advertised with a simple painted notice and a number to call.

"Every man has a right to a Saturday night bath."

- Lyndon B. Johnson

82

IMBIBE SOME CRAZY WISDOM

Drukpa Kunley, also known as the 'Divine Madman', came from Tibet to Bhutan in the fifteenth century. A tantric master, he spread his profane 'crazy wisdom' throughout the country, scandalizing those who heard his rude verses, but doing so in order to shake people out of their habitual and unthinking practice of Buddhism. One of his most famous exploits is his taming of the Long Rong demoness by thrusting his 'flaming thunderbolt' into a rock in which she had hidden; it is said that the fragments of the rock can still be seen by the Puna Tsang Chu River. His biography and verses are collected in *The Divine Madman* (translated by Keith Dowman), and provide a fresh and surprising take on Buddhism!

"I am the sun at its zenith and upon whatever continent I shine I cast no shadow."

- Drukpa Kunley

83

CIRCUMAMBULATE THE NATIONAL MEMORIAL CHORTEN

The National Memorial Chorten in Thimphu is a pleasant spot to slow down and recharge. Visible both day and night from some distance, it is particularly beautiful in the evening. From early morning throughout the day people come to meet and visit with friends, and to circumambulate the chorten. This gentle activity gives the location a sense of peace and community: either do a few slow laps yourself (clockwise, as always), or join some of the elderly locals on a bench, toss crumbs to the pigeons, and watch the gentle action unfold.

"Until he extends his circle of compassion to include all living things, man will not himself find peace."

- Albert Schweitzer

84

FIND THE 'MOST EXCELLENT HIGH BRIDGE'

There are dozens of bridges on the National Highway, and some of the larger ones have names proclaiming their own qualities. The Most Excellent High Bridge, not to be confused with the Strong and High Bridge on the same road, is in a particularly beautiful spot. To give as clue as to its location: you will have to stop there anyway…

"Praise the bridge that carried you over."

- George Colman

85

GET "FRESH" WITH A ROADSIDE VENDOR

Fruits and vegetables in season, fresh curd, and local cheese are sold on roadsides all over Bhutan. Bargaining is not traditionally part of the Bhutanese culture so prices are not inflated to allow for discounting. The produce is organic, and may not look perfect as in Western super markets, but fresh Bhutanese fruits and vegetables taste great and the seller is probably the grower. The small cherry-sized tomatoes in particular are like putting a small circus in your mouth!

"Taste every fruit of every tree in the garden at least once. It is an insult to creation not to experience it fully."

- Stephen Fry

86

GIVE SOMETHING BACK

For all that Bhutan is trying to develop in accordance with the model of Gross National Happiness, the country does have its problems. Find a way to give one or two hours of your time to help Bhutan as it searches for a balance between tradition and modernity, and between spirituality and material necessity. Your investment will pay off well in the future.

"The best way to find yourself is to lose yourself in the service of others."

- Mahatma Gandhi

87

LOOK OVER THIMPHU DZONG AT NIGHT

Thimphu Dzong, also known as Tashichhodzong, is the administrative centre of Bhutan. The civil service is based there, the King has his own office, and it hosts ceremonial events of national import. The building, like most *dzongs*, is of course impressive. However, for the best view, take a ride out towards the suburb of Taba at night. The *dzong* is lit up in white and red, and the road out to the north of the city provides a superb view of it.

"I'd rather live in a cave with a view of a palace than live in a palace with a view of a cave."

- Karl Pilkington

88

SUCK ON THE HARD CHEESE OF BHUTAN

Do not try to chew this cheese! Dentists in Bhutan are few and far between. The dice-sized dry cheese cubes are strung together and sold at the roadside shops. A distraction on lengthy treks, it will keep you from getting thirsty. It takes hours to soften in your mouth, during which time it tastes and feels like a small piece of granite. It won't spoil during your lifetime so take some home with you if you like. Enjoy!

"I don't want the cheese, I just want to get out of the trap."

- Spanish Proverb

89

ROCK AND ROLL

One of the most fascinating aspects of Bhutan is the interplay between tradition and modernity. While many younger Bhutanese have embraced the modern in the form of music, the country's own identity is never abandoned, and as such is it not unusual to see a Bhutanese in a *gho* or *kira* rocking out to some Dzongkha pop, to some Indian metal, or to the good old Beatles. To get to the heart of the capital's music scene, pay a visit to Mojo Park – the country's first dedicated live music venue – on Chang Lam.

"Without music, life would be a mistake."

- Friedrich Nietzsche

90

ENJOY SOME LOSAR HOSPITALITY

The Bhutanese celebrate Losar in early spring. It is the lunar new year, but with attached Buddhist significance. Families gather to eat together, and if you are invited to a Losar dinner, you will also find yourself plied with more cups of *ara* than you can possibly drink. The Bhutanese use the Chinese zodiac of twelve animals, but each year is also assigned a gender and an element: the year 2010, for example, was the year of the male iron tiger. Each year is considered either auspicious or inauspicious for various activities, so take the opportunity to find a lama who can tell you whether this is a good time to marry, move house, or start a business.

"Eating, and hospitality in general, is a communion, and any meal worth attending by yourself is improved by the multiples of those with whom it is shared."

- Jesse Browner

91

FOLLOW A MASK DANCE

The central attractions of *tshechus* are the spectacular mask dances. Some are performed by monks and others by lay people, but in each case every movement has great significance. It is worth researching one or two of the dances in order to gain a better sense of the meaning of the performance.

"The human face is, after all, nothing more nor less than a mask."

- Agatha Christie

92

WATCH TRADITIONAL HANDICRAFTS BEING MADE

The Bhutanese take immense pride in their handicrafts. These are not relics of the past, and the hand-woven fabrics, devotional *thangkha* paintings, and wooden masks still play a large role both in daily life and in rituals that still have great importance. In total, there are thirteen branches of handicrafts. Jewelers can be seen at work on the east side of the river in Thimphu, while the National Institute of Zorig Chusum, commonly known as the painting school, provides an opportunity to see artisans at work. Master artisan Phuntso Wangdi, former instructor at the Institute, and onetime official palace painter to the royal family, can be found painting in Buddha Handicrafts across from the prayer wheel in Paro.

"The life is short, the craft so long to learn."

- Hippocrates

93

COUNT THE PRAYER FLAGS AT CHELE-LA

Although more difficult to access than Dochu-la (see #21), Chele-la is in fact the highest drivable pass in Bhutan. Chele-la lies on the road between Paro and the northwestern town of Haa at an altitude of 13,084ft (3,988m). It is a fantastic spot at any time, with great views of the high peaks of the Himalayas during the day, and shooting stars often visible at night – if you are willing to brave the cold! Counting the prayer flags there could take a lifetime but give it a try, and when you get deep into three figures you can stop counting and revel in just 'being'.

"*Despite all I have seen and experienced, I still get the same simple thrill out of glimpsing a tiny patch of snow in a high mountain gully and feel the same urge to climb towards it.*"

- Edmund Hillary

94

PASS EASTWARDS THROUGH NYALA LUNMA

Traveling to remote eastern Bhutan takes time, so much so that it is difficult to do justice to it in a single trip. However, the long journey is worth the effort: it is less developed than the west of the country, and very different in character. Anyone travelling east along the national highway must pass though Nyala Lunma on the stretch between Wangdue Phodrang and Trongsa. Author and folklorist Kunzang Choden records that this dark and forbidding spot is home to a demoness. To ensure smooth passage, she advises travelers to acknowledge the demoness, but not to request anything of her…

"And the end of the fight is a tombstone white, with the name of the late deceased,
And the epitaph drear: 'A fool lies here who tried to hustle the East.'"

- Rudyard Kipling

95

LEARN TO COOK A BHUTANESE DISH

Bhutan is not known to be an epicurean oasis of delight. In fact, some of the most frequently heard comments made by foreigners is that the food lacks variety. It is also the case that, while most of the world regards chilies as a seasoning, the Bhutanese see them as a vegetable and staple food. As such, much of the food is so spicy as to be inedible. However, it is certainly possible to enjoy extraordinary meals comprised solely of traditional Bhutanese dishes. Learning to prepare such dishes will probably entail an invitation into a private home, and which dishes are prepared will depend on the availability of seasonal ingredients. The memorable aspects of learning to cook Bhutanese food will more than likely be in the social interaction and conversation than in the meal itself.

"A good cook is a certain slow poisoner, if you are not temperate."

- Voltaire

96

GET STONED BY A MONKEY

That's 'by', not 'with', however tempted you may be by #53. Monkeys live in many areas of Bhutan, predominantly in the south but also in some valleys at lower altitudes. Frequently spotted along the national highway, they will beg for food from passing vehicles. They have also been known to shuffle around the hillsides causing loose rocks to roll down towards humans walking on the road: whether this is intentional or not is known only to them...

"We are just an advanced breed of monkeys on a minor planet of a very average star. But we can understand the Universe. That makes us something very special."

- Stephen Hawking

97

COMPARE TRADITIONAL AND CONTEMPORARY ART

Contemporary art in Bhutan is developing in fascinating ways. VAST (Voluntary Artists' Studio, Thimphu) is home to some incredibly talented artists who often take traditional art and supply a modern twist. In order to get a sense of the traditions on which they are drawing, examine traditional art in the form of *thangkha* paintings or symbolic scenes which only specially trained artisans are sanctioned to create. Painting on the inside and outside of homes and buildings is common, as are wall hangings painted on rice paper or parchment and framed with colored fabrics.

"Paintings have a life of their own that derives from the painter's soul."

- Vincent van Gogh

98

RECEIVE BLESSINGS AT DAWN

At many *tshechus*, a giant *thangkha* painting, bearing the image of Guru Rinpoche, is unfurled before dawn. It is believed that simply viewing the image bestows great blessings upon the viewer: reason enough to set your alarm clock!

"For the mind disturbed, the still beauty of dawn is nature's finest balm."

- Edwin Way Teale

99

PACK YOUR HIKING BOOTS

Bhutan is a hiker's dream, with views in abundance, diverse flora and fauna, and picturesque monasteries to aim for at the end of most walks. Treks can be demanding, however, with the combination of altitude and acute gradients meaning that even short treks can be a shock to the system for the un-acclimatized. From the popular Druk Path Trek between Thimphu and Paro, to the spectacular Jomolhari Trek, to the extreme, twenty-five day Snowman Trek, Bhutan presents a great range of options for walkers.

"Jumping from boulder to boulder and never falling, with a heavy pack, is easier than it sounds; you just can't fall when you get into the rhythm of the dance."

- Jack Kerouac, **The Dharma Bums**

100

WALK FURTHER

While formal treks like those mentioned above are certainly worth doing, walking has its own significance in Bhutan. The national highway linking east and west Bhutan was completed in the 1960s, and the widespread use of motorized transportation is a fairly recent development. For most of the country's history, travel was on foot or on the back of a donkey; only a generation ago, some Bhutanese were renowned for the huge distances they were able to cover. There's no better place on earth for walking, with limitless fresh air and stunning views. We recommend that you walk when you could ride, and always try to go a little further as there is usually something spectacular just round the corner or over the next peak. You'll be glad you did…

"Come, come quickly. Let's walk. For health. Fresh air is there."

- D.G. Lhato Jamba

… and in the spirit of going further, we offer you some additional items for your *Bhutan Bucket List*. Bhutan just can't be done in 100!

More items are given in the following pages, and we invite you to venture a guess as to why there are exactly eight more.

101

FIND THE FOURTH KING'S FOOTBALL BOOTS

The Royal Heritage Museum, spectacularly located in the watchtower above Trongsa Dzong, contains an interesting and eclectic mix of royal and national memorabilia. As the museum's name suggests, items tend to focus on the royal family, and include the soccer boots worn by the Fourth King as a teenager. It also contains items of religious and historical significance, including 500-year old items belonging to Yongzin Ngagi Wangchuk, the founder of Trongsa Dzong, and a biography of Guru Rinpoche written by his consort.

"It's a lovely experience walking around a museum by yourself."

- Brad Pitt

102

EXPERIENCE BHUTAN'S FLORA IN A SINGLE AFTERNOON

When travelling through Bhutan, it often feels as if each valley has its own eco-system. The extremes of altitude between the Indian plains and the high peaks of the Himalayas mean that the country is home to a spectacular array of plants and animals. While there is no substitute for seeing flora and fauna in their natural habitat, the Royal Botanic Gardens on the edge of Thimphu provide a handy shortcut for plant lovers. The gardens are worth a visit in their own right: a popular picnic spot amongst locals, they are beautifully landscaped, with a bamboo garden, a dedicated orchid display, water features, and pleasant views of Thimphu valley.

"Beauty surrounds us, but usually we need to be walking in a garden to know it."

- Rumi

103

DON'T HOG THE MIC!

If you don't manage to get yourself invited to a singalong (see #39), you will at least have the chance to sing karaoke. As in much of Asia, this is a popular evening pastime, with participants fairly unselfconscious about their tunefulness or otherwise. The mixture of songs available is, however, unusual, with a choice of Hindi, Nepali and Bhutanese hits being the staple for karaoke-goers. Most places tend to have one or two English numbers available, which is good news if you feel moved to join in, but don't expect too much choice… and if you find yourself enjoying it, make sure you relinquish the mic!

"Sometimes I do need to go to karaoke, sometimes I need to relax."

- Jackie Chan

104

HELP OUT WITH A LANDSLIDE CLEARANCE

Landslides are part of life in Bhutan, and resulting delays on the roads are common. They are particularly frequent in the rainier summer months, although some areas are prone to rockfalls all year round (see #10). If you do find yourself delayed by a slide, you may as well pitch in and help: you won't be going anywhere until the road is clear anyway.

"Gravity is a habit that is hard to shake off."

- Sir Terry Pratchett, **Small Gods**

105

CATCH A GAME AT CHANGLIMITHANG

Bhutan's national stadium, known as Changlimithang, is located in central Thimphu; many of the tourist hotels on Chang Lam directly overlook it. The stadium's architecture is distinctively Bhutanese, with one side of the pitch home to a pavilion for members of the Royal family, Ministers and VIPs, with the other side occupied by larger terraces for ordinary fans. Changlimithang burst into life in the Spring of 2015, when Bhutan – then the lowest-ranked soccer team in the world – shocked Sri Lanka to secure a place in the Asian qualifying rounds for the 2018 World Cup. If you are able to, catch either one of the World Cup qualifying games or any other event at the national stadium as it is a uniquely picturesque location for international fixtures.

"You can't put a limit on anything. The more you dream, the farther you get."

- Michael Phelps

106

EXPERIENCE THE MONSOON

Bhutan has a monsoon climate, with heavy rainfall between the months of June and September, although the weather varies depending on location. While not as heavy as the monsoon elsewhere, notably India, the rains are nevertheless spectacular, and can cause havoc on the roads as they tend to produce landslides. The rains give Bhutan a completely different character and visitors the opportunity either to admire the low-hanging clouds from comfort or to head out and experience the rains head-on, preferably on a mountainside.

"Rain is grace; rain is the sky descending to the earth; without rain, there would be no life."

- John Updike

107

CHECK THE QUIRKY ROAD SIGNS

Most roads in Bhutan are built and maintained by Project DANTAK, part of the Indian Army Corps of Engineers. One might assume that the presence of sheer drops of hundreds of meters, often only inches away from your vehicle's wheels, would be reminder enough of the need for road safety in these parts, but the engineers of DANTAK nevertheless erect signs providing helpful safety hints. The tone of these signs straddles uncertain territory, ranging from the whimsical, (Mountains are Pleasure only if you Drive with Leisure) to those verging on the dark (This is Highway, not Runway). We've given you these two for starters: if you can make it to a dozen, you will have covered a lot of road whilst proving to be observant!

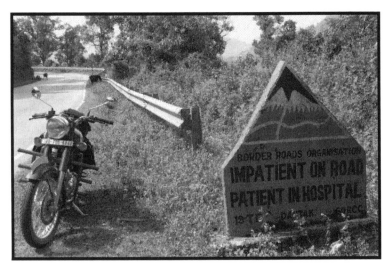

"Better to be Mr. Late than late Mister."

- DANTAK road safety sign

108

Describe Bhutan Without Using the words 'Shangri-la', 'Pristine' or 'In the Clouds'

Part of the pleasure of a trip is sharing the experience. Bhutan is so overwhelming that it is often difficult to know where to start, and it will take some imagination to describe what you see, feel and experience while in Bhutan. Give it some thought and post your comments on The Bhutan Bucket List Facebook page. Thanks and *Tashi Delek*!

"Prose is architecture, not interior decoration, and the Baroque is over."

- Ernest Hemingway

GLOSSARY

Ara   Home-brewed Bhutanese liquor.

Bodhisattva   Sometimes translated as 'saint', a
                     bodhisattva is one who is determined
                     to achieve enlightenment in order to
                     benefit all other sentient beings.

Buddha   The historical figure referred to as
                     Buddha was Siddhārtha Gautama,
                     born in what is now southern Nepal
                     and attaining enlightenment at Bodh
                     Gaya. However, the term 'Buddha'
                     refers to any enlightened being. There
                     are, therefore, numerous Buddhas, all
                     of whom have their special qualities.
                     These characteristics are reflected in
                     their depictions in statues and *thangkha*
                     paintings.

Chorten   A representation of Buddha's mind.
                     Also called 'stupas' elsewhere, these
                     vertical monuments can range in size
                     from tiny to building-sized.

Chu   Water. Can also refer to river (running
                     water) and rain (falling water).

Datsi   A traditional Bhutanese dish made
                     with cheese sauce.

Drukpa Kunley   Also known as the 'divine madman'.
                     Drukpa Kunley arrived in Bhutan

from Tibet in the 15th century. A tantric master, he is known for his bawdy verses and shocking behavior.

Dzong A combination and fortress and monastery, these spectacular buildings serve as administrative centers.

Dzongkhag An administrative region. There are currently twenty dzongkhags in Bhutan.

Emas Chilies. Present in large numbers in most Bhutanese dishes.

Gho The national dress for men. It is a floor-length robe, worn hitched up to the knees and secured with a belt.

Guru Rinpoche The founder of Buddhism in Bhutan. An 8th century master, also known as Padmasambhava.

Kira Part of the national dress for women. A straight, woven, floor-length skirt.

Lhakhang Monastery.

Lam The Bhutanese word for 'street'.

Losar Lunar new year as celebrated in Bhutan and Tibet.

Lozey A traditional form of ballad.

Pema Lingpa The most famous *terton*, or treasure finder.

Puja	A Buddhist religious ritual.
Tashi Delek	A traditional greeting used in both Bhutan and Tibet. Its meaning is difficult to translate directly, but it bestows luck and blessings.
Tego	Part off the national dress for women. A silk blouse.
Terma	A sacred text or artefact, hidden by Guru Rinpoche for later generations for find.
Terton	A treasure finder. One who discovers the sacred texts and artefacts hidden by Guru Rinpoche.
Tshechu	Religious festivals, famous for their mask dances. Tshechus are held across Bhutan at different times of the year.
Thangkha	A Buddhist devotional painting. The emphasis is not on artistic originality, but in reproducing and accurately representing the religious subject matter, which is often the image of a Buddha or Bodhisattva.

Notes, Musings, Observations and Contact Info for New Friends

When? Where was it? Who was there? Who Said What? What was it like?

_____

_____

_____

_____

_____

_____

_____

_____

_____

_____

_____

_____

_____

_____

_____

_____

_____

_____

About the Authors

Professor Rob Marjerison (pictured right) is a former merchant mariner and satellite telecommunications executive. Seeking change, he joined the faculty at the Royal University of Bhutan and spent the following four and a half years riding a vintage motorbike through the Himalayas and teaching in the Business Department at Royal Thimphu College.

Stavan Attwood (pictured left) comes from northeastern England. He has spent much of his career abroad teaching at universities in Africa, China, Thailand and South Korea before arriving in Bhutan in January 2014. He holds a doctorate in English literature, and teaches literature at Royal Thimphu College.

Other titles in The Official Bucket List Series

Beware of cheap imitations.

Accept no substitutes!

Made in the USA
San Bernardino, CA
04 October 2015